BRAND LIKE A

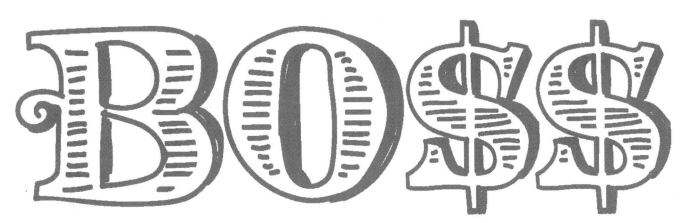

BRAND LIKE A BOSS

AN INTERACTIVE WORKBOOK

BY OLORI SWANK

THIS BRAND BELONGS TO:

_____

CONTENTS

CONTENTS (CONT.)

INTRODUCTION

Welcome! You're here! You did it! You took step one.

What is step one? Step one is showing up. Step one is making the decision to be better. Step one is making the commitment to do the work.

Perhaps you already have a brand and you want to get deeper into the branding of it. Maybe you are just starting your brand and you have no idea where to begin. Regardless of your experience level, cultivating a solid brand can be incredibly intimidating and overwhelming. Fret not, I am here to help.

About a decade ago, I stuck my toe in the entrepreneurship pool, and I was a fish out of water to say the least. Most of the time I had no idea what I was doing or if I was doing anything right. I didn't know if my ideas would make me millions or make me homeless. I was scared, confused, and oftentimes frustrated. Sometimes I was able to get a few answers from more seasoned entrepreneurs, but most of the time I was relying on the grace of God and the results of a million Google searches.

Since then, I have gone on to not only create a few successful brands, I've become a brand myself. Recognized by other major brands like CNN, Forbes, Vogue, Essence, and Huffington Post to mention a few; I think it's safe to say I've learned a few things along my journey.

I created this workbook as a roadmap and guide to help you in creating the brand of your dreams. This workbook is the book I wish I would have had when I first started; so I created it for you - I want you to win with it!

With that being said, this workbook is not a magic spell or replacement for hard work. True success will only be achieved if you take the information you gather here and do the work. So DO THE WORK! I'm rooting for you!

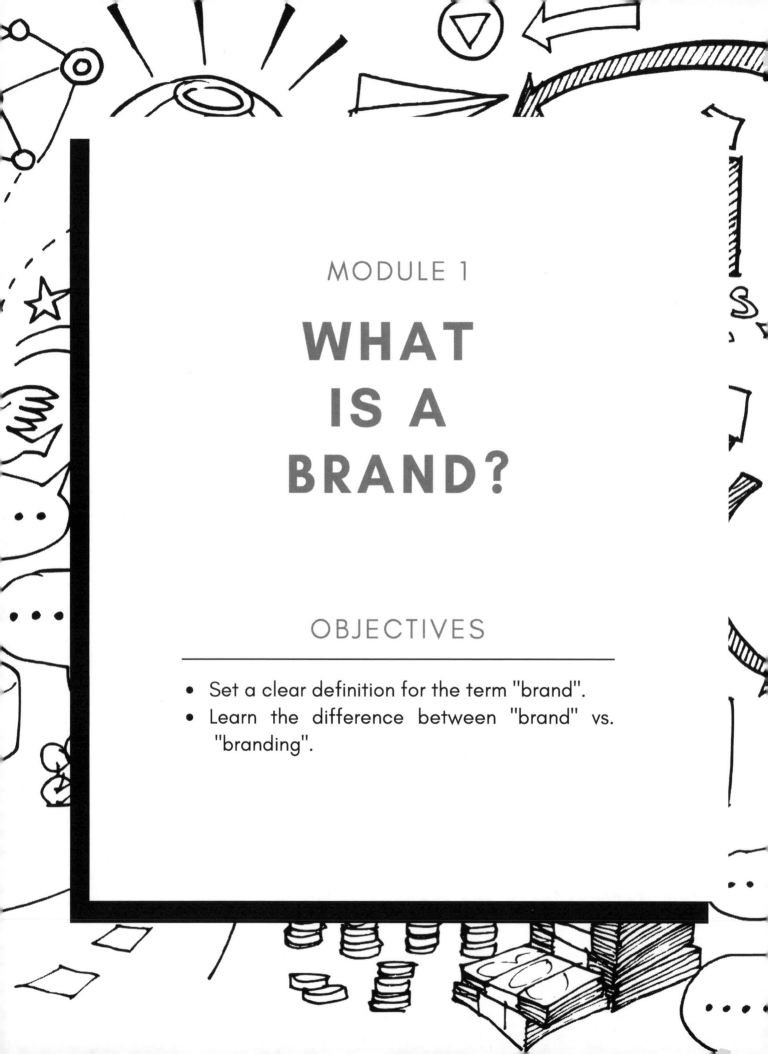

MODULE 1

WHAT IS A BRAND?

OBJECTIVES

- Set a clear definition for the term "brand".
- Learn the difference between "brand" vs. "branding".

> **A brand is no longer what we tell the consumer it is, it is what consumers tell each other it is.**
>
> — SCOTT COOK

TERMS TO KNOW

Brand
The impression people have of your business; the way your business is perceived.

Branding
1. The action of developing your brand. 2. Tactics and strategies you can use to influence how your brand is seen.

Brand Ambassador
The face, spokesperson, or representative of a brand. 2. a person who makes efforts to humanize brand messaging.

Brand Awareness
The extent to which consumers are familiar with the distinctive qualities of a particular brand of goods/services.

Brand Equity
The value your brand has on your business; can be a positive or negative value.

Brand Experience
The means by which a brand is created in the mind of a consumer through all interactions with the brand.

Brand Identity
1. The visual elements of your brand. 2. Logos, colors, typography, graphic components etc.

Brand Management
A continued analysis and execution of all techniques utilized to maximize the value of the brand over time.

Brand Strategy
The long-term strategy that guides a business in the development of a brand.

Brand Values
An unwavering declaration of values or promises that steers a brand toward its "true north."

Rebranding
When a brand owner revisits the brand with the purpose of updating or revising based on internal or external circumstances. Rebranding is often necessary if the brand has outgrown its former identity.

WHAT IS A BRAND?

When the average person hears the word "brand," they typically think of a logo, or a color palette. I say Nike, a swoosh comes to mind. Target, a bulls eye. Even if I were to say Tiffany & Co., Starbucks, or Chanel, one would begin to envision logos and color combinations. But here's the thing, a brand is so much more than just a recognizable logo paired with a consistent use of a single color scheme. Yes, logos and colors do play a major role in brand identity but without the other elements that comprise a "brand," logos are useless and hold no real value.

If Nike wasn't consistent in their brand language and lingo, if they didn't stick to their core values of inspiration and innovation, would the swoosh really mean anything? As a matter of fact, what if the swoosh logo belonged to another brand? Let's say it was the logo of your neighborhood dry cleaner. Do you think that just because the cleaner has the logo they will now become a global brand with the sales revenue to match?

Let me ask you to think deeper here for a moment. What else besides the swoosh do you think of when you hear the word, Nike? Maybe the "just do it" tagline. You might even get a mental picture of athletes, or champions, or thousands of kids standing in long lines the morning of every new release. Believe it or not, the imagery and thoughts that popped in your head are all a part of Nike's branding. Some of this is intentional – one of Nike's core values is "every athlete in the world'; and some of it is not. I'm sure Nike doesn't want the idea of camping out for sneakers and kids robbing each other for them to be a part of their branding, but unfortunately for them, it is. That's why being decisive in all areas that constitute your brand is so important. Whether positive or negative, the experience a person has with your brand will become a part of your brand identity.

So if a brand isn't just a logo and colors, then what is it exactly? A brand is a combination of look, tone, and the way the brand makes a consumer feel.

WHAT IS A BRAND?

Essentially, we can say a brand is the impression people have of your business. It is how they would describe your business if they were talking to a friend. Every business has a brand whether they take time to invest in branding or not. Take the post office for example. Their brand has become long lines, angry employees, and lost packages. Whether they like it or not, that's the brand they've established through their branding - or lack thereof. Which brings me to another definition. What is branding? Branding is the combination of action, tactics, and strategies you take in developing your brand. Think of your brand as the thing. Branding is the series of decisions you make to bring the thing into fruition. Consider branding as a plan of action taken in order to influence how your brand is seen. For example, if you want your brand to be perceived as high-end and exclusive, then things like invite-only events and premium packaging for your products will guide people into thinking that. Or let's say you want people to see your brand as relatable and approachable, then going live on Instagram and doing Q&A sessions will encourage people to think that. As I've stated before, everything must be considered when you're building a brand. The way you greet your customers, to how easy it is to find contact information on your website, to the size and feel of your business card will all influence the way a person sees your brand.

NOTES

_____

_____

_____

_____

_____

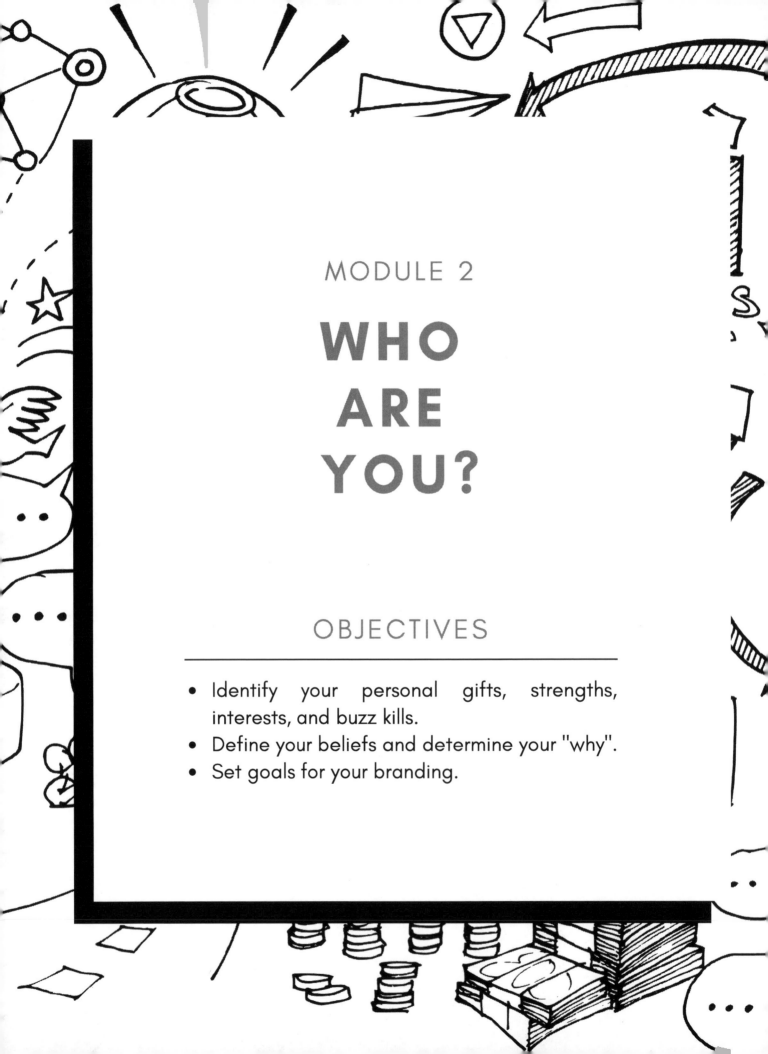

MODULE 2

WHO ARE YOU?

OBJECTIVES

- Identify your personal gifts, strengths, interests, and buzz kills.
- Define your beliefs and determine your "why".
- Set goals for your branding.

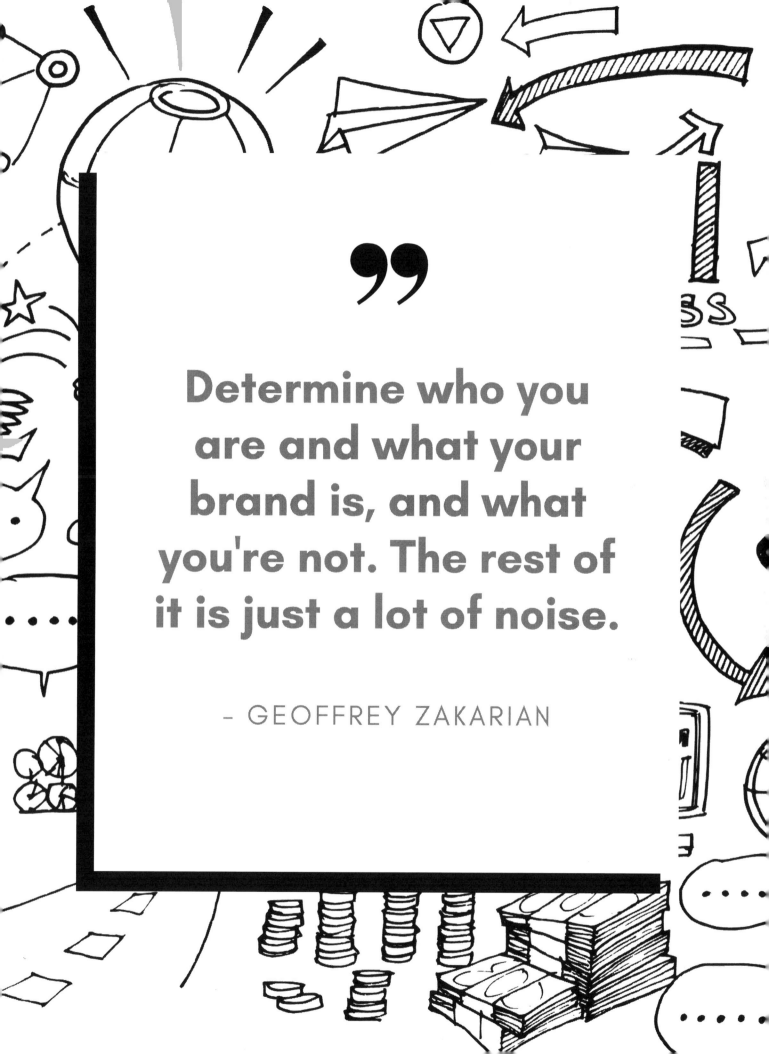

Determine who you are and what your brand is, and what you're not. The rest of it is just a lot of noise.

– GEOFFREY ZAKARIAN

YOUR GIFTS

01. What do you think you are naturally good at?

_____

_____

02. What do your friends and family consistently say you are good at?

_____

_____

03. What are your favorite things about yourself?

_____

_____

04. What lights you up and puts you in your zone?

_____

_____

05. What brings you down and annoys you?

_____

_____

YOUR BELIEFS + "WHY"

Take a moment to think about your favorite brand, celebrity, or influencer. I'm sure you can say one of the reasons you like them is because they stand for something bigger than just their own success. It's very possible that you also like them because they believe passionately in what they do, and those beliefs align with yours.

People want to buy into brands that stand for and believe in something. You are a major part of your brand, so what do you believe in?

What causes do you believe strongly in?

What does a "better world" look like to you?

YOUR BELIEFS + "WHY"

Who do you fight for?

Why do you do what you do?

How do you improve the lives of others?

YOUR BELIEFS + "WHY"

What impact do you aspire to have on your community?

What do you get excited about when doing business with a new customer?

What type of legacy would you like to leave?

BRANDING GOALS

To ensure a successful pass at properly branding your business, you must define some clear goals. Trying to brand your business without formulating goals is like getting in your car with no destination - you'll either waste gas driving in circles, or end up going nowhere because your car hasn't even moved yet.

By setting goals you'll not only be able to have units to measure the success of your branding, you'll also know where to concentrate more of your efforts.

Use the checklist below to brainstorm some goals for your branding. Don't limit yourself by thinking only about what you can achieve at the level you're at now. You can be forward-thinking and set goals that help you get to the level you want to be. A list of some has been provided below. Use the remaining space to brainstorm some of your own.

- [ ] increase your business's visibility online
- [ ] build a loyal tribe around your brand
- [ ] establish yourself as an authority in your space
- [ ] attract a new demographic of customers
- [ ] attract a new group of customers from your competitors
- [ ] increase your prices
- [ ] increase your sales revenue by selling more low-price products
- [ ] increase your sales revenue by selling fewer products at a higher price
- [ ]
- [ ]
- [ ]
- [ ]

NOTES / BRAINSTORMING PAGE

MODULE 3

WHO IS YOUR BRAND?

OBJECTIVES

- Create a clear brand personality.
- Determine your brands unique positioning (U.P.).
- Establish your brands core values.
- Find your brands niche products/services.
- Create an elevator pitch for your brand.

> **If people believe they share values with a company, they will stay loyal to the brand.**
>
> – HOWARD SCHULTZ

BRAND PERSONALITY

In the previous module you tapped into who you are, now let's tap into who your brand is.

If your brand were a person, what would he or she be like? Are they adventurous and bold? Demure and reserved? Or maybe they're glamorous and extraverted?

Establishing a strong brand personality will play a huge role in developing a solid brand presence. Customers want to connect with companies that align with their beliefs and speak to their personalities. Having a well thought out brand personality helps your customers connect and relate more to your business; ultimately helping to build brand loyalty because they will feel like they're interacting with a comrade rather than doing business with a faceless company.

In addition, knowing the personality of your brand will help you make easier decisions down the line when it comes to your brand collateral. Things like marketing campaigns, or even the verbiage used in your email correspondence will be cohesive because you know the personality of your brand.

Defining a clear and consistent brand personality while talking to your customer in a way they can relate to will help your customer realize that your brand is for them.

KEY POINTS

- Customers want to connect with companies that align with their beliefs and speak to their personalities.
- Knowing the personality of your brand will help you make easier decisions down the line when it comes to your brand collateral.

NOTES

ADJECTIVE ACTIVITY

A wonderful way to start defining your brand personality is by making a list of adjectives to describe your business.

Really dig deep and ask yourself how you want your brand to be perceived.

Is your brand more:

Fun or **Serious**   *Lavish* or **Essential**   *Relaxed* or **Formal**   *High-End* or **Everyday**

USE THE SPACE BELOW TO BRAINSTORM AS MANY ADJECTIVES AS YOU CAN TO DESCRIBE YOUR BUSINESS:

BRAND PERSONALITY EXAMPLES

Active	Humble	Reliable
Adventurous	Humorous	Respectful
Ambitious	Idealistic	Responsible
Calm	Imaginative	Romantic
Caring	Impressive	Rustic
Charismatic	Independent	Sarcastic
Cheerful	Innovative	Secure
Childish	Insightful	Sensitive
Clever	Kind	Sentimental
Competitive	Leaderly	Serious
Confident	Leisurely	Sexy
Creative	Lovable	Simple
Curious	Loyal	Sociable
Daring	Mature	Sophisticated
Dedicated	Modest	Spontaneous
Dignified	Neat	Stern
Dramatic	Optimistic	Stoic
Elegant	Outspoken	Stubborn
Energetic	Passionate	Stylish
Flexible	Patient	Suave
Focused	Peaceful	Sweet
Friendly	Playful	Trendy
Fun-loving	Polished	Trusting
Generous	Popular	Understanding
Genuine	Protective	Warm
Glamorous	Pure	Whimsical
Hardworking	Realistic	Witty
Honest	Relaxed	Youthful

BRAND AWARENESS

01. When someone first encounters your brand, what general impression do you want them to have of it?

_____

_____

02. After doing business with you, what are some things you would want clients to say about you, your products, or your brand?

_____

_____

03. Why is your brand a better fit for your customer than any other comprable brand on the market?

_____

_____

04. What is your ultimate goal for your brand? (Give your most 'wildest dreams' response)

_____

_____

05. What steps do you need to take in the next three months, six months, and year to get closer to accomplishing your ultimate brand goals?

_____

_____

BRAND AWARENESS

06. What will be some of your biggest obstacles in reaching your brand goals? (ex: time limitations, family obligations, lack of resources, etc)

_____

_____

07. What will be the most exciting part of reaching your ultimate brand goals?

_____

_____

08. How will you reward yourself once you accomplish your brand goals?

_____

_____

09. What grand promise is your brand making to your clients?

_____

_____

10. What benefit can your clients come to expect from every interaction with your brand?

_____

_____

UNIQUE POSITIONING (U.P.)

I'll be honest, the first time I ever heard the term "unique positioning," I was a bit intimidated. I had no idea what it meant and it sounded like something that would take me forever to figure out. Thankfully, determining your unique positioning is not as hard as you might think.

To put it in very simple terms, your unique positioning is the single message you push in your marketing to let people know what makes you different and sets you apart from your competitors.

Some examples of unique positioning can be high-quality, fast and efficient service, convenience, etc. Let's look at unique positioning statements from some of the world's leading brands:

COCA COLA

For individuals looking for high-quality beverages, Coca-Cola offers a wide range of the most refreshing options -- each creates a positive experience for customers when they enjoy a Coca-Cola brand drink. Unlike other beverage options, Coca-Cola products inspire happiness and make a positive difference in customers lives, and the brand is intensely focused on the needs of consumers and customers.
(U.P. = High Quality)

APPLE

Apple provides cutting edge technology for tech-savvy consumers who want the top of the line laptops, computers, and mobile devices. Apple promotes inclusion and accessibility for all and takes responsibility for its employees in addition to committing itself to sourcing the highest quality materials and products.
(U.P. = Advanced Technology)

UNIQUE POSITIONING (U.P.)

 CHIPOTLE

Chipotle provides premium, real ingredients for customers looking for delicious food that's ethically sourced and freshly prepared. Chipotle's dedication to cultivating a better world by cutting out GMOs and providing responsibly raised food sets them apart in the food industry. (U.P. = Premium Ingredients)

 AMAZON

For consumers who want to purchase a wide range of products online with quick delivery, Amazon provides a one-stop online shopping site. Amazon sets itself apart from other online retailers with its customer obsession, passion for innovation, and commitment to operational excellence. (U.P. = Fast Service)

As you can see, these brands have all chosen one area of focus to lead with in their marketing. Most of the time when you see an Amazon ad, it's promoting fast service; most Chipotle ads focus on the quality of their ingredients. This is because those are the qualities they established for their unique positioning. This doesn't mean that is the only thing they do well; or that no one else is doing the same thing. It just means that is what they've chosen to use to set themselves apart from the competition. Solid unique positioning is why the next time you want a quesadilla with premium ingredients, you'll go to Chipotle (v.s Taco Bell if you're looking for fast service).

UNIQUE POSITIONING (U.P.)

Now, it's your turn!

Use the space below to brainstorm some angles you would want to leverage in the marketplace by way of unique positioning.

_____

_____

_____

_____

_____

_____

_____

_____

_____

_____

_____

_____

_____

UNIQUE POSITIONING (U.P.)

PRODUCTS + SERVICES

01. What products do you sell or what services do you offer?

_____

_____

02. How many products/services will you offer initially?

_____

_____

03. If you were explaining your product/service to a child, how would you explain what you offer?

_____

_____

04. What are the tangible and intangible benefits of your product/service?

_____

_____

05. What's the process you use to create and deliver your product or service? Detail what it looks like from the first moment you encounter a client, to the moment they receive their product/service.

_____

_____

PRODUCTS + SERVICES

06. Will people buy your products or book your services online, in stores, or both?

07. How will you distribute your products or render your services?

08. Where will you store your products or perform your services? Will you need to rent office/storage space or do you have a spare room in your house?

09. Will you be working with a manufacturer, buying wholesale, or making your products yourself?

10. What are the costs associated with producing your product or rendering your services? (Don't forget to include time and money).

PRODUCTS + SERVICES

11. How will you determine the pricing of your products/services?

_____

_____

12. Which of your products/services get the best reviews? What do your customers say about them?

_____

_____

13. What products/services do you plan to add in the future?

_____

_____

14. What's your favorite part of creating and delivering your product/service?

_____

_____

15. What's your least favorite part of creating and delivering your product/service?

_____

_____

CORE VALUES

As I've mentioned several times already, building a brand involves several components. It's about the colors you choose for your packaging, the way your store smells, the experience a customer has browsing your website, and even the tone you use when communicating. Branding is about the promises you make to your customers and what they can come to expect from your brand. As you can see, there are so many moving parts to this wheel of branding. To ensure all these components are cohesive, you must have a well-established foundation that all of these things stem from. That foundation is your core values.

Your core values will set the tone for how you present your brand to the world and the standards at which you operate. The values you hold to the highest regard will dictate what makes your brand unique and play a huge role in how you serve the marketplace. Say for example one of your core values is creativity. Creativity will cause you to have pop-up business cards rather than traditional ones. Creativity will cause you to create mind-blowing photo booths and installations in your retail store so that your customer is wowed with their overall experience. Creativity will cause you to send thank-you videos to your customers rather than just sending hand-written notes. The values you choose will come to dictate so much of what you do and how you do it. For this reason, it's important to look within and ask yourself what your core values are.

It doesn't stop there. A well-defined set of core values will also help your customers relate better to your brand. Kind of like how having a well-defined brand personality does. Having the same values as them will play a significant role in encouraging customers to be loyal to your brand. A set of shared values lets them know that the things important to them are also important to you. You will be able to develop a relationship with them built on trust and understanding because they know you're on the same page as them.

CORE VALUES

When it comes to choosing your core values, my tip is to take it a step beyond just a basic word choice. Put the words into action by asking yourself how your brand will exercise that particular value. Values like "dependability" and "kindness" sound great, but do they actually make your brand unique? Or do they also describe every other business in your industry?

If "gratitude" is the core value you choose, go beyond the obvious by explaining how it is your business will be grateful? Having a core value like, "Always eager to serve our clients from a place of gratitude" already sounds better than simply "gratitude". Elaborate! That's how you can create a clear message and build a memorable brand.

NOTES

_____

_____

_____

_____

_____

CORE VALUES ACTIVITY

01. What things matter to you the most?

02. What things do your competitors seem to slack on?

03. What are some things your customer will say makes you different?

04. What are some things you're not willing to skimp on regardless of effort/budget?

05. What does the perfect experience with your business look like to a customer?

CORE VALUE EXAMPLES

Accessibility
Activeness
Adaptability
Adventure
Ambition
Balance
Beauty
Bravery
Care
Change
Communication
Confidence
Control
Craftsmanship
Creativity
Dependability
Devotion
Dignity
Discretion
Ease of use
Education
Enjoyment
Entertainment
Environment
Equality
Excitement

Family
Fitness
Freedom
Freshness
Friendship
Fun
Goodwill
Gratitude
Growth
Guidance
Happiness
Health
Humor
Imagination
Individuality
Innovation
Inspiration
Intelligence
Kindness
Leadership
Learning
Mindfulness
Motivation
Optimism
Originality
Passion

Patience
Peace
Playfulness
Positivity
Potential
Power
Pride
Productivity
Quality
Relationships
Reliability
Respect
Safety
Security
Sharing
Simplicity
Speed
Stability
Strength
Success
Support
Sustainability
Trust
Understanding
Uniqueness
Warmth

NOTES / BRAINSTORMING PAGE

THE ELEVATOR PITCH

The ability to articulately explain what you do and why you do it will be another important role in your brand building process. There's nothing worse than being in a room full of people and not being able to tell people what you and your brand are all about in a clear, succinct manner.

Before you find yourself in that type of conundrum, let's craft an "elevator pitch" to help you win people over with your passion and poise. Use the space below to draft a quick and clear speech about what you and your brand are all about.

Keep in mind that it's called an 'elevator pitch' because you shoud be able to deliver the whole speech in the length of an elevator ride (typically 60 seconds or less). Keep it short, sweet, and very much to the point.

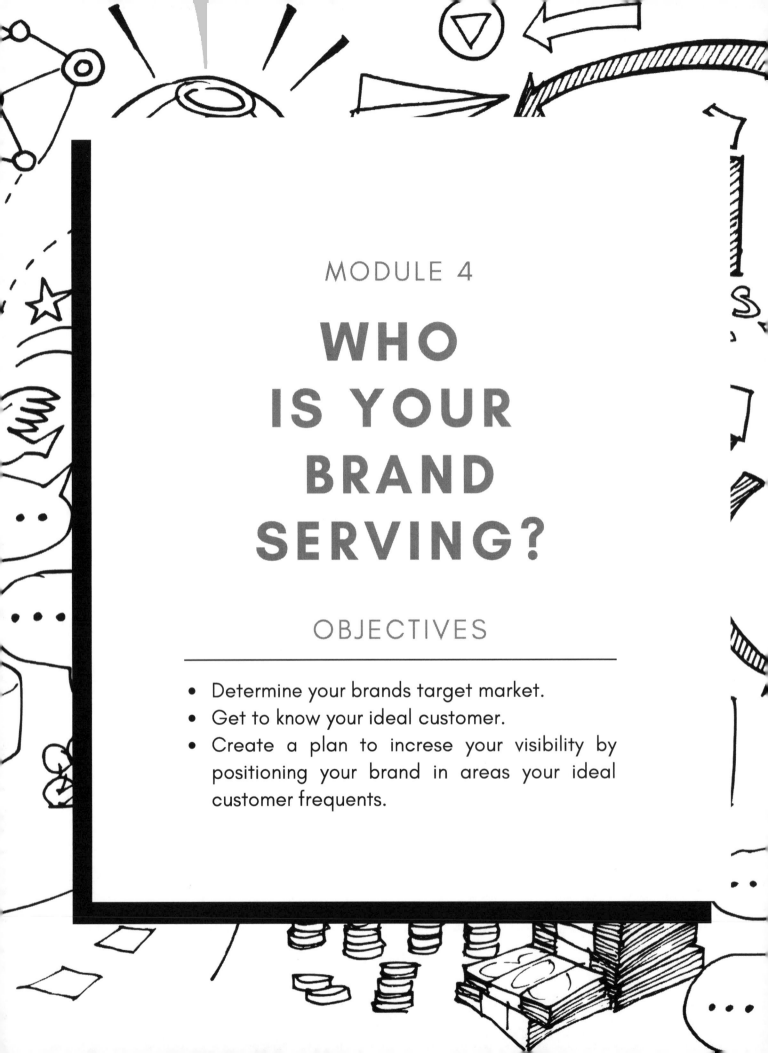

MODULE 4

WHO IS YOUR BRAND SERVING?

OBJECTIVES

- Determine your brands target market.
- Get to know your ideal customer.
- Create a plan to increse your visibility by positioning your brand in areas your ideal customer frequents.

Your brand is what other people say about you when you're not in the room.

– JEFF BEZOS

TARGET MARKET

One of the biggest mistakes I see with many business owners (especially the new ones) is that they try to make their product or service cater to everyone. This typically will then cause them to use vague wording in their messaging, take less risks in their offerings, and have a list of services that is entirely too long. Taking the route of catering to everyone is a huge mistake! Defining a target audience and establishing an ideal customer is a major component of branding. Rather than keeping a broad, undefined range of target consumers, it's essential that you drill down and hone in on the precise kind of customers you want to serve.

This may sound scary at first because as a new business owner you just want to get customers. You may feel like niching down will cause you to lose potential clients; but let me give you a personal story to help bring this home for you. In my early years of business, I was making a name for myself as a fashion stylist, but I was also good at garnering press for self and curating events. I figured I could do all three professionally. For that reason, on my first business card, my company line read that we specialized in, "fashion styling, event planning, and public relations" – don't laugh. Looking back on that business card, I now realize why no one was coming to me for any of those services. People want to deal with companies that are focused and have an area of expertise. If you cater to everyone and offer everything, people will not come to you for anything. They will much rather pick the company that they know is great at what they're in search of. There's a reason Apple doesn't sell washing machines and refrigerators – I'm just saying.

Even if you possess a wide range of skills, it's usually far more profitable to focus on one thing and become an expert in it than to

TARGET MARKET

chase multiple rabbits and never catch any. By being more discerning of the type of customer that you want to attract, you'll be equipped to fine-tune your offerings; and be laser-focused on what you need to do to create a brand that attracts the kind of audience you're looking for. All this will eventually lead to a stronger brand.

Complete the questions below to get a better understanding of the type of customer you want to target.

What is the problem they want to be solved?

What are their pain points?

What are their internal barriers?

TARGET MARKET

What are their external barriers?

How does the problem they face affect their daily lives?

How does your company help solve their problem?

NOTES

ACTION ITEMS

- As you answer each question, brainstorm how your brand can be a solution. How do you make the lives of those in your target market better? Remember, the best brands are answers to a question or solutions to an existing problem.

IDEAL CUSTOMER AVATAR

Use the following pages to help you further identify the traits and preferences of your dream customer. Every customer will not fit this mold exactly so consider this chart to be a guide or baseline of what a member of your target audience might look like. You may also want to make more than one customer avatar if you have multiple customer types that fit your niche.

Gender + Age

Ethnicity

Location

Education Level

Occupation + Income

Children

Marital Status

IDEAL CUSTOMER AVATAR

Interests:

Hobbies:

Passions:

Personality:

IDEAL CUSTOMER AVATAR

Values:

Social Issues He/She Cares About:

How He/She Practices Self Care:

Dream Vacation:

IDEAL CUSTOMER AVATAR

Types of Books He/She Reads:

Types of Magazines He/She Enjoys:

Types of Blogs He/She Subscribes To:

Most Frequently Used Social Media Platforms:

IDEAL CUSTOMER AVATAR

What Would Make Him/Her Trust a New Brand?

What Is His/Her Primary Concern In Life?

How Does He/She View The World?

What Outlet Does He/She Prefer To Share Recommendations On? (text message/email/social media/etc)

IDEAL CUSTOMER AVATAR

What Does He/She Save For?

What Does He/She Splurge On?

What Is His/Her Biggest Monthly Expense?

What Is His/Her Favorite Affordable Expense/Purchase?

IDEAL CUSTOMER AVATAR

Favorite Food

Favorite Restaurant

Favorite Celebrity

Favorite Brands

Favorite T.V Show

Favorite Place

Favorite Car

Favorite Social Media Platform

Favorite Electronic Device

Favorite Form of Communication

Favorite Sport

Favorite Movie

Favorite Season

Favorite Emoji

IDEAL CUSTOMER AVATAR

Introvert or Extravert

Serious or Playful

Cats or Dogs

City or Suburbs

Coffee or Tea

Laptop or Tablet

Salty or Sweet

Beach or Mountains

Instagram® or Facebook®

Snapchat® or Twitter®

Brunch or Happy Hour

Name Brand or Generic

SUV or Coupe

Traditional or Modern

ASK YOUR AUDIENCE

Paying attention and asking your audience the right questions will always give you better insight and help you gain the information necessary to meet your overall objective in serving your consumer. Keep your questions open-ended and center them around the types of things that you need to know in order to help them. Examples of areas of focus might be: what motivates them; what frustrates them; what do they struggle with; what are they lacking; etc. Come up with 20 open-ended questions that you can ask your audience to gain this valuable insight.

01.

02.

03.

ASK YOUR AUDIENCE

04.

_____

_____

05.

_____

_____

06.

_____

_____

07.

_____

_____

08.

_____

_____

ASK YOUR AUDIENCE

09.

10.

11.

12.

13.

ASK YOUR AUDIENCE

14.

_____

_____

15.

_____

_____

16.

_____

_____

17.

_____

_____

18.

_____

_____

ASK YOUR AUDIENCE

19.

20.

BRAND VISIBILITY

If a tree falls in the forest and no one is around to hear it, does it make a sound? That's the adage that comes to mind when I think of the many people who take the time to create brand guides and strategy, but don't devise a plan on how and where to implement them. Deciding who to target is just as important as knowing where to be to get on their radar. Are you showing up in the right places to get seen?

Use the space below to give your brand a better chance at being seen.

What places does your brand show up?

What formats do you use to engage your audience?

BRAND VISIBILITY

What incentives does your brand use to gather testimonials & referrals?

List some dream brand ambassadors you would love to hire for your brand.

What outlets are your brand most advertised in?

MODULE 5

WHAT DOES YOUR BRAND LOOK LIKE?

OBJECTIVES

- Create a Brand Style Guide (complete with logo, color pallete, typography, etc) that will serve as a rule book and map for the visual representation of your brand.

When you look at a strong brand, you see a promise.

– JIM MULLEN

BRANDING ELEMENTS

Now that we've done the work to define the core essence of your brand and what it stands for, we can begin to create a physical identity for your brand that will translate these values in a tangible way. This is what we will refer to as "branding."

In the process of branding, you will create a name, design a logo, and identify a color palette, amongst other things. The choices you make in this branding process will play a major role in setting your company apart from others.

REMEBER

- Branding is deeper than just a logo.
- Look + Tone + Feel = Branding.
- Branding is a tool you use to differenciate yourself from other brands.

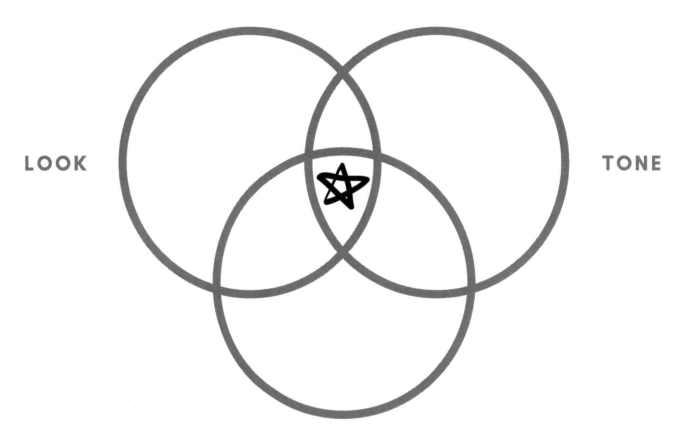

LOOK

TONE

FEEL

 = BRANDING

BRAND NAME CHECKLIST

☐ **01. Your brand name is easy to spell and remember.**
Being creative with your brand name will set you apart; however, you don't want to be creative to the point that your brand name becomes too complicated. Keep it easy to spell and remember.

☐ **02. Your brand name is well-suited for your target audience.**
Choose a name that will resonate well with the type of customer you're looking to attract. It may help to ask for feedback from clients, fellow business people, and anyone you know that fits your target market.

☐ **03. Your name is not already being used by a similar brand.**
A simple google® search could help you determine this. While doing so, also make sure there are not any other brands with a similar name that have a bad reputation.

☐ **04. Your brand name is not already a registered trademark.**
Checking before you decide to use it can save you from finding yourself in a future lawsuit &/or having to change your name. Search this by using the United States Patent and Trademark Office electronic search system: http://www.uspto.gov/trademarks/

☐ **05. Your brand's domain name and social media handles are available.**
Namecheckr.com is a great site to use to check multiple domain extensions and social media platforms at once.

NOTES

_____

_____

BRAND STYLE GUIDE

Think of a brand style guide as a roadmap that will be used to create a cohesive look across all outlets and channels. By taking the time to create a brand style guide, you can ensure that the core essence of your brand is properly translated into design. Answer the questions below to get started:

What is your brand identity currently lacking? What areas do you think your brand identity can improve in?

What areas do you think your current brand identity is strong in?

BRAND STYLE GUIDE

Write your mission statement below:

Write your vision below:

Write a short description of your dream client below:

FIND INSPIRATION

Sometimes it helps to start by getting inspired. List the domain names of a few websites you find visually appealing. Try to find similarities in all of them. In addition, narrow down any specific characteristics/features that you really love about each one.

DOMAIN NAMES	SIMILARITIES + CHARACTERISTICS
1.	
2.	
3.	
4.	
5.	
6.	
7.	

VISUAL STYLE ASSESMENT

Which terms best describe your visual style preferences? Please use the scales below to rate your disposition.

FEMININE ——— ○ ——— ○ ——— ○ MASCULINE

LIGHT ——— ○ ——— ○ ——— ○ DARK

BRIGHT ——— ○ ——— ○ ——— ○ NEUTRAL

CALM ——— ○ ——— ○ ——— ○ ENERGETIC

SIMPLE ——— ○ ——— ○ ——— ○ COMPLEX

QUIRKY ——— ○ ——— ○ ——— ○ TRADITIONAL

FORMAL ——— ○ ——— ○ ——— ○ CASUAL

LUXURY ——— ○ ——— ○ ——— ○ AFFORDABLE

What physical objects would you say reflect your brands energy?
(e.g., plants, coffee, champagne, crystals, etc.)

FONTS + TYPOGRAPHY

Finding the perfect fonts to use in your branding can be a tedious and daunting task. There are so many different types to chose from. In this guide, I've broken them down into 6 basic categories (note: There are many more category types that can be made. This list is NOT all-inclusive). Read the descriptions of each to familiarize yourself with the various options and then using the examples on the following page, circle the style that resonates with you best.

Serif. A serif is a small line or stroke regularly attached to the end of a larger stroke in a letter or symbol. Serif fonts have been around forever. Because of their long history, people tend to be more trusting of text written in a serif font. The classic nature of a serif font often lends validity to your words in the eye of the reader. The most popular serif font is Times New Roman.

Sans Serif. "Sans" means "without," so like their name implies, sans serif fonts are fonts without serifs. You won't find any of the tiny strokes at the end of sans serif fonts. As opposed to a serif font, the missing strokes give a sans serif font an overall modern, minimalist, clean look. Popular sans serif fonts include Helvetica, Avant Garde, and Arial.

Theme. Theme fonts are fun, quirky, and attention-grabbing. They tend to evoke a greater sense of feeling from the reader. It can be anything from the nostalgia of attending movies as a child, to the feelings of terror and suspense when you come ac-

NOTES

FONTS + TYPOGRAPHY (CONT.)

ross a gory font. Since life has a ton of different themes, there are also a ton of different types of theme fonts. It's best to use theme fonts as headers; they can be quite difficult to read in the body of text.

Handwriting. Handwriting fonts were created with the intent to resemble someone's writing. Being that handwriting varies from person to person, handwriting fonts can also look vastly different from font to font. Handwriting fonts are also good for establishing rapport and trust with the reader. The benefit to using this type of font is it's more approachable and less intimidating than other fonts. They tend to work well for more casual or homemade brands.

Script. Script fonts also come in a wide range of styles. These typefaces also mimic handwriting but they're more elegant and sometimes formal - think cursive and calligraphy. Script fonts are perfect for invitations and special occasion announcements.

Gothic. Gothic fonts have been around for quite some time and are inspired from the Middle Ages. Although the name might give off the connotation of fear, that's not the case here at all. Consider gothic fonts to be a no-nonsense typeface.

NOTES

FONTS + TYPOGRAPHY

BRAND LIKE A BOSS

Sans Serif

BRAND LIKE A BOSS

Serif

BRAND LIKE A BOSS

Theme

BRAND LIKE A BOSS

Handwriting

Script

BRAND LIKE A BOSS

Gothic

FONTS + TYPOGRAPHY

There is a world of fonts just waiting to be explored. Using the space below, find some fonts you love. Visit sites like: dafont.com, myfonts.com, fontsquirrel.com, google.com/webfonts, and write out the fonts that speak to you. Don't forget to make note of where you found them in the adjacent spaces.

Font Name

Font Source

Font Name

Font Source

Font Name

Font Source

Font Name

Font Source

Font Name

Font Source

Font Name

Font Source

FONTS + TYPOGRAPHY

Font Name

Font Source

Font Name

Font Source

Font Name

Font Source

Font Name

Font Source

Font Name

Font Source

Font Name

Font Source

Font Name

Font Source

COLORS

Selecting a color palette for your brand goes way beyond simply choosing your favorite color. It is not enough to choose the color pink as your brand color merely because you're a girly-girl and the color makes you happy. There's actually a great deal of psychology that goes into color and the way it affects consumer behavior.

With that being said, the best practice would be to make sure the message you're aiming to send with your color choice aligns with your customers expectations. Keep in mind that the same color can symbolize different things. For example, to one person the color yellow could mean caution, while meaning joy and happiness to another. This is why it is important to look at color as a single element that will work with other brand elements to deliver your message; versus making the mistake of thinking your customer will know what you're trying to convey based on color alone.

It also helps to make sure you are not sending mixed messages with your color choices. If you sell baby clothes but the colors on your site are forest green and mahogany brown, your brand is sure to be mistaken for one that sells camping equipment. The earthy, rugged connotation of the color combination will definitely cause some confusion.

As you decide which colors to use in your branding, make sure that you're brainstorming from a place of what you want your customers to perceive, rather than the personal preferences you have for yourself.

NOTES

COLOR PSYCHOLOGY
POSITIVE & NEGATIVE

 white

CLEAN	STERILITY
PURITY	COLDNESS
SIMPLICITY	UNFRIENDLY
CLARITY	ISOLATION

red

ENERGY	AGGRESSION
FEARLESSNESS	ANGER
POWER	DANGER
PASSION	WARNING

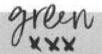 **gray**

UNCONFIDENT	NEUTRALITY
DAMPNESS	RELIABILITY
LACK OF ENERGY	BALANCE
BLANDNESS	INTELLIGENCE

orange

ENERGETIC	FRUSTRATION
FUN	IMMATURITY
FRIENDLY	IGNORANCE
WARMTH	DEPRIVATION

green

NATURAL	BOREDOM
FRESH	ENVY
HEALTH	STAGNATION
GROWTH	SICKNESS

yellow

OPTIMISTIC	IRRATIONALITY
YOUTHFUL	ANXIETY
ATTENTION-GRABBING	FRUSTRATION
HAPPINESS	CAUTION

 blue

TRUST	COLDNESS
SECURITY	ALOOFNESS
TRANQUILITY	EMOTIONLESS
INTELLIGENCE	UNFRIENDLINESS

purple

WISDOM	DECADENCE
LUXURY	SUPPRESSION
WEALTH	MOODINESS
ROYAL	INTROVERSION

brown

FRIENDLY	HEAVINESS
WARMTH	SADNESS
SERIOUSNESS	DIRTINESS
RELIABILITY	UNSOPHISTICATED

 pink

IMAGINATIVE	FLIPPANCY
PASSION	IMPULSIVENESS
CREATIVE	ECCENTRICITY
FEMININE	NONCONFORMITY

black

SOPHISTICATION	OPPRESSION
SECURITY	COLDNESS
POWER	EVIL
AUTHORITY	MOURNING

gold

WEALTH	SHREWDNESS
VALUE	ARROGANT
WISDOM	MATERIALISTIC
COURAGE	OBSESSIVE

CHOOSING COLORS

A great place to find inspiration for your color palette is coolors.co.

The site has thousands of pre-made color schemes for you to explore. You can also use their generator to create more individualized color schemes. Simply click "start the generator," then press the space bar continuously until you find a color you like. Once you find the color your you like, hover your cursor over the color and click the padlock icon. This will ensure that color remains in your color grid. Press the space bar again to change all the unlocked colors. Every time the tool generates a color you like, lock it in place using the padlock and press the space bar to change the remaining colors. Continue these steps until you love all the colors and the overall scheme.

Write the 6-character HEX color code for each color you have selected below. Knowing the HEX color code will ensure any designer you hire will use the exact color consistently.

PRIMARY COLOR PALETTE

Designers and developers use HEX colors in web design.
A HEX color is expressed as a six-digit combination of numbers and letters defined by its mix of red, green and blue (RGB).

#abc123   #abc123   #abc123   #abc123   #abc123

LOGO

Throughout this guide I've made mention that branding is more than just a logo. These statements were not to coerce you into forgoing a logo; or half hazardly creating one for that matter. Logos may not be the only element of branding, but they are a pretty important one. Consider your logo to be the face of your brand. It's typically the most identifiable component of your brand, so you should put some thought into creating one.

For a logo to serve its purpose, it needs to function on white backgrounds, as well as inverted out on black backgrounds; in a single color as well as in full color. Your logo has to be legible when it's enlarged to the size of a billboard, and also the size of your thumbnail. When I meet new entrepreneurs, a lot of them want so many elements in their logo. I've heard requests of adding a full illustration of a woman doing hair, to hiding images inside the logo text. Imagine shrinking these logos int the size of a clothing label. Those details will not only be lost, the logo will most likely be illegible and messy. For best practices, keep your logo clean and free from clutter. Try not to use elements that are too trendy or will date your logo. The objective is for your logo to have an impact while remaining simple. Think of brands like Nike, Apple, Gap, Chanel and Target, these brands are massive and their logos are clean and to the point.

With that being said, how much should you pay for a good logo? The answer here is not to get caught up on price. I have logos I've paid $500+ for, as well as logos I paid less than $30 for. They are both great. Most days I actually like the $30 logo better than all other logos. Not because it was the most friendly on my pockets, but because it's the one I spent the most time researching and being intentional about before hiring someone to create it. You should do the same.

LOGO

Before hiring a designer (or doing your logo yourself), there are some things to keep in mind:

- Your logo should be clean, unique, and memorable.
- Avoid any trendy elements that will easily cause your logo to look outdated.
- Select a logo that will stand out from your competitors while also still being appropriate for your target audience.
- Do not break the bank on logo design. It's important to have a professional logo but it's not ok to have no money left over for your brand after creating a logo.

Sites like fiverr.com and 99designs.com are great for hiring freelancers at an affordable price. Canva is perfect for a DIY option. Just remember when hiring a designer to create your logo that you take some time to share your brand message and core values with them. Giving them a deeper understanding of your brands purpose will help them better create a logo that sends the message.

LOGO

PRIMARY LOGO

Your primary logo is the main graphic that represents your business and is used most often. When designing the primary logo, your goal is to communicate who you are, what you offer, or where you operate. This logo may include your company's tagline, website, or geographic location.

LOGO VARIATIONS

Sometimes referred to as a secondary logo, a logo variation is a different version of your primary logo. For example, if your primary logo is in a horizontal format, sometimes space doesn't always allow those exact dimensions so you use a variation. Below are some variations for my brand, SWANK Blue®.

 S W A N K   B L U E

SKETCH YOUR LOGO/IDEAS

SKETCH YOUR LOGO/IDEAS

1-PAGE BRAND BOARD FORMAT

LOGO

LOGO VARIATIONS

COLOR PALETTE (HEX CODES)

#abc123   #abc123   #abc123   #abc123   #abc123

FONTS

FONT NAME

ABCDEFGHIJKLMNOPQRSTUVWXYZ
abcdefghijklmnopqrstuvwxyz
0123456789

FONT NAME

ABCDEFGHIJKLMNOPQRSTUVWXYZ
abcdefghijklmnopqrstuvwxyz
0123456789

IMAGERY

WHAT DOES YOUR BRAND SOUND LIKE?

OBJECTIVES

- Establish a tone for your brand.
- Create buzz words for your brand.

> **Define what your brand stands for, its core values and tone of voice, and then communicate consistently in those terms.**
>
> — SIMON MAINWARING

ACTIVITY: WRITE A LETTER

Let's pretend you spot your dream client sitting accros from you in a cafe or lounge. You want to introduce yourself and your brand but it is very crowded and loud so you will have to write a letter. In the space below, write down what you'd say to that person.

ACTIVITY: WRITE A LETTER

BRAND VOICE

Analyze the letter you wrote to your dream client and answer the questions below:

Describe the tone of voice you used in your letter? Were you formal or casual? Friendly or straight-to-the-point? Take a moment to really describe the vibe of your letter.

Based on what you know about the characteristics of your target market, do you think the tone of your letter will make them confident to engage with your brand?

What vibe do you want to communicate with your brand? Does the tone of your letter match the vibe? If not, what changes can you make to improve the tone?

BUZZWORDS

If you're a brain surgeon that specializes in operating on patients with life-threatening ailments, greeting them with "Hey Cutie," in your email correspondence is not going to go over well. Such action may also cause them to lose confidence in your expertise.

It is important to ensure that your messaging aligns with what your target audience wants. Take a moment to identify buzzwords that you can use repeatedly to establish a consistent brand voice.

USE THE SPACE BELOW TO BRAINSTORM AS MANY BUZZWORDS AS YOU CAN TO USE IN YOUR COMUNICATION AND MARKETING:

WHAT DOES YOUR BRAND FEEL LIKE?

OBJECTIVES

- Create objectives, processes and the policies necessary for your customer to have the ultimate customer experience.

> A brand is the set of expectations, memories, stories and relationships that, taken together, account for a consumer's decision to choose one product or service over another.

— SETH GODIN

BRAND FEEL

The way your brand makes a customer feel (good or bad) is a large component to branding. This single component is essentially what will establish your brands reputation in the marketplace. The brand "feel" is the reason we love eating at Chic-fil-A and dread going to the Department of Motor Vehicles (DMV). The DMV has established a reputation for being a nightmare of a place simply because they never took the time to decide how to make their customers "feel" good while engaging with their brand. Whereas, a company like Chic-fil-A prides themselves on the customer experience and has even created a concept that they call, "second mile service". They are committed to going the extra mile to make their customers feel valued. In turn, we've all come to know the Chic-fil-A brand as one that makes it's customers feel good.

Creating a good "feel" for your brand doesn't necessarily have to be expensive. It just requires a great deal of intentionality. You must take into account the customers experience with everything from your customer service to ease of navigation on your website. Even something as simple as the smell of your retail location can affect the customer experience.

In this module you will make decisions and establish protocol for the components that affect the way a customer feels when engaging with your brand.

KEY POINTS

- Creating a good "feel" for your brand doesn't necessarily have to be expensive. It just requires a great deal of intentionality.
- You must take into account the customers experience with everything from your customer service to ease of navigation on your website.

NOTES

CUSTOMER SERVICE

01. What is the attitude your customers experience from you and your team members?

02. How quickly to do respond to customer emails &/or return phone calls? How long is a customer on hold if they call your business?

03. How fast do you ship customer orders or deliver their products? If you provide a service, how soon are you available to service the average client?

04. How often do you make changes and adjustments based on customer complaints and feedback? How much does their opinion matter to you?

05. What steps do you take to rectify any mistakes you make or problems your customer has? How fast do you make the correction?

CUSTOMER SERVICE

06. What is your return policy? How long does the customer have to return items they are dissatisfied with?

_____

_____

07. How can customers monitor the status of their order? Do you send emails throughout the entire delivery process?

_____

_____

08. Do you follow up with customers after they've recieved a product or service to guage their level of satisfaction?

_____

_____

PRODUCT EXPERIENCE

01. What is the quality of your product or service? (very high, high, average, below average, poor)

_____

_____

02. How durable and long-lasting are your products or how long do the results of your services last?

_____

_____

03. How effiecient are your products or services? Do customers find that it improves the qualty of their life?

_____

_____

04. Does your product or service actually do what your brand promises it will do? Are your customers satisfied?

_____

_____

05. What value do customers gain from purchasing your product or services? Would they brag about the value to their friends?

_____

_____

ONLINE EXPERIENCE

01. Is your website clean and free from clutter? How easy is it to navigate? Are customers able to find what they're looking for easily?

_____

_____

02. How easy is it to read the fonts on your site? Is there enough contrast between the font color and background color to easily read the text?

_____

_____

03. Are your customers bombarded with ads and pop-ups? How hard is it to opt-out of ads or close pop-up windows?

_____

_____

04. Is your contact info easy for the customer to locate? Do you have any chat features enabled? If so, how long does it take to get a response?

_____

_____

05. How secure is your site? What security does your site have in place to protect customer payment information?

_____

_____

IN-PERSON EXPERIENCE

01. Is your physical location clean and easy to navigate? How hard is it for customers to find what they are looking for?

_____

_____

02. Is the location of your store/office/etc easy to access/find? When customers arrive is it easy to find parking? If not, do you offer valet?

_____

_____

03. Do you have furniture for customers/clients to utilize while in your space? Is this furniture visially appealing? Is the furniture comfortable?

_____

_____

04. Is the vibe right? Is the lighting in your physical location condusive for the type of product or service you offer? What does your space smell like?

_____

_____

05. What ammenities can visitors of your space enjoy? Do you offer free wi-fi, water, magazines, or coffee?

_____

_____

PERSONAL TOUCHES

Sometimes the smallest things make the biggest impact. Gestures like hand-written thank you cards and personal phone calls can go a very long way. Even acts as simple as walking your clients out to their car or including a small gift in their online order can make a huge difference in how they see your brand. Use the space below to brainstorm personal touches that will create joyful moments for your customers.

PERSONAL TOUCHES

MODULE 8

BRANDING TOUCH POINTS

OBJECTIVES

- Determine intended uses of your brand identity.

> **Your brand is a story unfolding across all customer touch points.**
>
> – JONAH SACHS

BRANDING TOUCHPOINTS

Every interaction and/or occasion a consumer comes in contact with your brand is called a touchpoint. Touchpoints are important because they serve as an opportunity to bring awareness to your brand. Consider a touchpoint as an opportunity to make a great first impression; or even remind someone who is already familiar with your brand that you exist.

Once you have created a solid foundation and identity for your brand, you need do develop touchpoints. A list of some has been provided below. Use the remaining space to brainstorm some of your own.

TOUCHPOINTS

- ☐ business cards
- ☐ brochures
- ☐ flyers
- ☐ letterheads
- ☐ proposals
- ☐ packaging
- ☐ blogs
- ☐ websites
- ☐ infographics
- ☐ videos
- ☐ presentations
- ☐ mobile apps
- ☐ social media platforms

- ☐ billboards
- ☐ signage
- ☐ print ads
- ☐ T.V. ads
- ☐ web ads
- ☐ email newsletters
- ☐ youtube
- ☐ illustrations
- ☐ stickers
- ☐
- ☐
- ☐
- ☐

RESOURCE

BRANDING CHECKLIST

OBJECTIVES

- Complete the checklist to ensure you've covered all your branding bases.

A brand is essentially a container for a customer's complete experience with the product or company.

– SERGIO ZYMAN

BRAND LIKE A BOSS CHECKLIST

☐ **Identify your gifts.**
Knowing your strengths will help you pinpoint areas to focus your energy on. It will also help you determine where to outsource.

☐ **Determine your "why".**
Why you do it will always determine 'how' you do it. Learning your 'why' early will save you a lot of headache.

☐ **Write your mission statement.**
A clear message stating how and why you serve your customers daily will help you stay on track.

☐ **List your brand values.**
Well-defined core values will ensure your company works collectively towards a shared vision.

☐ **Set some goals.**
One of the single-most important things you can do to help the success of your brand and branding is to set goals.

☐ **Set some boundaries.**
A lot of opportunities will come your way on your journey. Make a list of what you'll accept and what you'll turn down.

☐ **Establish a core offering.**
Identify your core product or service and create messaging around it that speaks to your target customer

☐ **Define your target audience.**
You shouldn't try to be everything to everyone. Identify a niche and aspire to be a leader in it.

☐ **Give your brand a persona.**
Figure out your brand personality. This will attract an audience that genuinely connects with your brand.

☐ **List keywords for your brand.**
Make a list of brand keywords to use throughout your copy to help boost your search engine optimization rankings.

BRAND LIKE A BOSS CHECKLIST

☐ **Design a mood board.**
A mood board is a collection of visuals that will aide in keeping the aesthetic of your brand consistent.

☐ **Find your brand fonts.**
Explore different fonts and typography to find the ones that speak most to the tone of your brand.

☐ **Settle on a website design.**
Explore web design options and land on one that ties the look, tone, and feel of your brand together.

☐ **Take professional headshots.**
Whether you are the face of your brand or not, there will come a time where press or collaborations will request one.

☐ **Create a social media strategy.**
Decide which platforms you will use and the content you will provide on each.

☐ **Design your logo.**
Do it yourself or hire someone to do it. Keep your logo clean, simple and timeless. Do not go overboard with small elements.

☐ **Choose your brand colors.**
Choose a color palette that supports the message your brand aims to send and evokes the appropriate emotions.

☐ **Acquire Brand Assets.**
Secure your domain name and the matcing email addresses. Get business cards, flyers, brochures, etc., made.

☐ **Secure your social media handles.**
Even if you don't plan on using the platform, make sure you secure your name on it.

☐ **Build your email newsletter.**
Choose a service to use to gather email subscribers and create a strategy to grow your list.

TO-DO LIST

TASKS	PRIORITY	DUE DATE	
			☐
			☐
			☐
			☐
			☐
			☐
			☐
			☐
			☐
			☐
			☐
			☐
			☐
			☐
			☐
			☐
			☐
			☐
			☐
			☐
			☐

TO-DO LIST

TASKS	PRIORITY	DUE DATE	
			☐
			☐
			☐
			☐
			☐
			☐
			☐
			☐
			☐
			☐
			☐
			☐
			☐
			☐
			☐
			☐
			☐
			☐
			☐
			☐
			☐

BRANDING VENDOR LIST

OBJECTIVES

- Create a directory of vendors and companies to outsource design work, printing, etcetera, from.

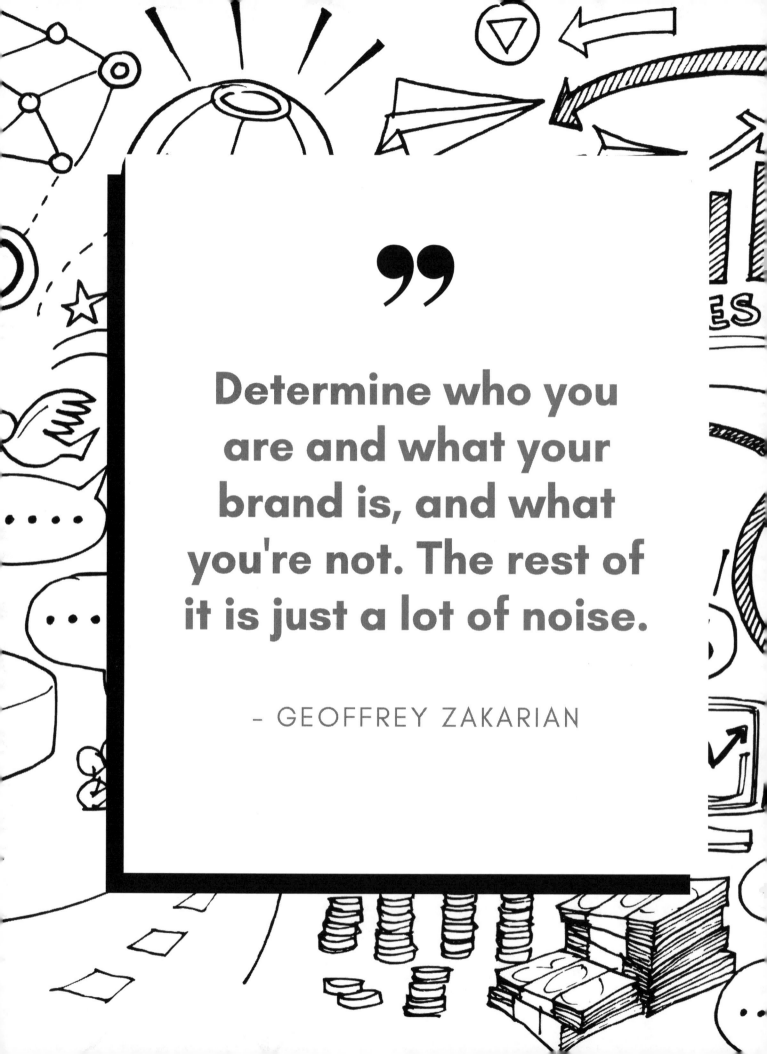

Determine who you are and what your brand is, and what you're not. The rest of it is just a lot of noise.

– GEOFFREY ZAKARIAN

BRANDING VENDOR LIST

Company: _____

Service Offered: _____

Address: _____

Contact Person: _____

Email: _____

Phone Number: _____

Website: _____

Company: _____

Service Offered: _____

Address: _____

Contact Person: _____

Email: _____

Phone Number: _____

Website: _____

Company: _____

Service Offered: _____

Address: _____

Contact Person: _____

Email: _____

Phone Number: _____

Website: _____

Company: _____

Service Offered: _____

Address: _____

Contact Person: _____

Email: _____

Phone Number: _____

Website: _____

BRANDING VENDOR LIST

Company: _____

Service Offered: _____

Address: _____

Contact Person: _____

Email: _____

Phone Number: _____

Website: _____

Company: _____

Service Offered: _____

Address: _____

Contact Person: _____

Email: _____

Phone Number: _____

Website: _____

Company: _____

Service Offered: _____

Address: _____

Contact Person: _____

Email: _____

Phone Number: _____

Website: _____

Company: _____

Service Offered: _____

Address: _____

Contact Person: _____

Email: _____

Phone Number: _____

Website: _____

BRANDING VENDOR LIST

Company: _____

Service Offered: _____

Address: _____

Contact Person: _____

Email: _____

Phone Number: _____

Website: _____

Company: _____

Service Offered: _____

Address: _____

Contact Person: _____

Email: _____

Phone Number: _____

Website: _____

Company: _____

Service Offered: _____

Address: _____

Contact Person: _____

Email: _____

Phone Number: _____

Website: _____

Company: _____

Service Offered: _____

Address: _____

Contact Person: _____

Email: _____

Phone Number: _____

Website: _____

BRANDING VENDOR LIST

Company: _____   Service Offered: _____

Address: _____

Contact Person: _____   Email: _____

Phone Number: _____   Website: _____

Company: _____   Service Offered: _____

Address: _____

Contact Person: _____   Email: _____

Phone Number: _____   Website: _____

Company: _____   Service Offered: _____

Address: _____

Contact Person: _____   Email: _____

Phone Number: _____   Website: _____

Company: _____   Service Offered: _____

Address: _____

Contact Person: _____   Email: _____

Phone Number: _____   Website: _____

BRANDING VENDOR LIST

Company: _____

Service Offered: _____

Address: _____

Contact Person: _____

Email: _____

Phone Number: _____

Website: _____

Company: _____

Service Offered: _____

Address: _____

Contact Person: _____

Email: _____

Phone Number: _____

Website: _____

Company: _____

Service Offered: _____

Address: _____

Contact Person: _____

Email: _____

Phone Number: _____

Website: _____

Company: _____

Service Offered: _____

Address: _____

Contact Person: _____

Email: _____

Phone Number: _____

Website: _____

BRANDING EXTRAS

OBJECTIVES

- Use these tools to aid in consistency and scheduling

YEARLY STRATEGIES

JANUARY

FEBRUARY

MARCH

APRIL

MAY

JUNE

JULY

AUGUST

SEPTEMBER

OCTOBER

NOVEMBER

DECEMBER

MONTHLY PLANNER

MONTH

SUN	MON	TUE	WED	THU	FRI	SAT

IMPORTANT DATES

IMPORTANT TASKS

"Tomorrow belongs to the people who prepare for it today."
- *African Proverb*

MONTHLY PLANNER

SUN	MON	TUE	WED	THU	FRI	SAT

IMPORTANT DATES

IMPORTANT TASKS

_____

_____

_____

"Tomorrow belongs to the people who prepare for it today."
- African Proverb

MONTHLY PLANNER

SUN	MON	TUE	WED	THU	FRI	SAT

IMPORTANT DATES

IMPORTANT TASKS

"Tomorrow belongs to the people who prepare for it today."
- *African Proverb*

MONTHLY PLANNER

MONTH

SUN	MON	TUE	WED	THU	FRI	SAT

IMPORTANT DATES

IMPORTANT TASKS

_____

_____

_____

"Tomorrow belongs to the people who prepare for it today."
- African Proverb

MONTHLY PLANNER

MONTH

SUN	MON	TUE	WED	THU	FRI	SAT

IMPORTANT DATES

IMPORTANT TASKS

_____

_____

_____

"Tomorrow belongs to the people who prepare for it today."
- African Proverb

MONTHLY PLANNER

MONTH

SUN	MON	TUE	WED	THU	FRI	SAT

IMPORTANT DATES

IMPORTANT TASKS

_____

_____

_____

"Tomorrow belongs to the people who prepare for it today."
- African Proverb

MONTHLY PLANNER

MONTH

SUN	MON	TUE	WED	THU	FRI	SAT

IMPORTANT DATES

IMPORTANT TASKS

"Tomorrow belongs to the people who prepare for it today."
- *African Proverb*

MONTHLY PLANNER

MONTH

SUN	MON	TUE	WED	THU	FRI	SAT

IMPORTANT DATES

IMPORTANT TASKS

"Tomorrow belongs to the people who prepare for it today."
- *African Proverb*

MONTHLY PLANNER

MONTH

SUN	MON	TUE	WED	THU	FRI	SAT

IMPORTANT DATES

IMPORTANT TASKS

_____

_____

_____

"Tomorrow belongs to the people who prepare for it today."
- African Proverb

MONTHLY PLANNER

MONTH

SUN	MON	TUE	WED	THU	FRI	SAT

IMPORTANT DATES

IMPORTANT TASKS

"Tomorrow belongs to the people who prepare for it today."
- African Proverb

MONTHLY PLANNER

MONTH

SUN	MON	TUE	WED	THU	FRI	SAT

IMPORTANT DATES

IMPORTANT TASKS

_____

_____

_____

"Tomorrow belongs to the people who prepare for it today."
- *African Proverb*

MONTHLY PLANNER

MONTH

SUN	MON	TUE	WED	THU	FRI	SAT

IMPORTANT DATES

IMPORTANT TASKS

"Tomorrow belongs to the people who prepare for it today."
- *African Proverb*

30-DAY CHALLENGE

1	2	3	4	5
6	7	8	9	10
11	12	13	14	15
16	17	18	19	20
21	22	23	24	25
26	27	28	29	30

30-DAY CHALLENGE

1	2	3	4	5
6	7	8	9	10
11	12	13	14	15
16	17	18	19	20
21	22	23	24	25
26	27	28	29	30

30-DAY CHALLENGE

1	2	3	4	5
6	7	8	9	10
11	12	13	14	15
16	17	18	19	20
21	22	23	24	25
26	27	28	29	30

30-DAY CHALLENGE

1	2	3	4	5
6	7	8	9	10
11	12	13	14	15
16	17	18	19	20
21	22	23	24	25
26	27	28	29	30

30-DAY CHALLENGE

1	2	3	4	5
6	7	8	9	10
11	12	13	14	15
16	17	18	19	20
21	22	23	24	25
26	27	28	29	30

PURPOSE/GOAL: _____

30-DAY CHALLENGE

1	2	3	4	5
6	7	8	9	10
11	12	13	14	15
16	17	18	19	20
21	22	23	24	25
26	27	28	29	30

WEEKLY PLANNER

MON

TUE

WED

THU

FRI

SAT

SUN

WEEK OF

TOP TASKS

NOTES

"Think ahead. Don't let day-to-day operations drive out planning."
- Donald Rumsfeld

WEEKLY PLANNER

MON

TUE

WED

THU

FRI

SAT

SUN

WEEK OF

TOP TASKS

NOTES

"Think ahead. Don't let day-to-day operations drive out planning."
- Donald Rumsfeld

WEEKLY PLANNER

MON

TUE

WED

THU

FRI

SAT

SUN

WEEK OF

TOP TASKS

NOTES

"Think ahead. Don't let day-to-day operations drive out planning."
— *Donald Rumsfeld*

WEEKLY PLANNER

MON

TUE

WED

THU

FRI

SAT

SUN

WEEK OF

TOP TASKS

NOTES

"Think ahead. Don't let day-to-day operations drive out planning."
- Donald Rumsfeld

WEEKLY PLANNER

MON

TUE

WED

THU

FRI

SAT

SUN

WEEK OF

TOP TASKS

NOTES

"Think ahead. Don't let day-to-day operations drive out planning."
- *Donald Rumsfeld*

WEEKLY PLANNER

MON

TUE

WED

THU

FRI

SAT

SUN

WEEK OF

TOP TASKS

NOTES

"Think ahead. Don't let day-to-day operations drive out planning."
- Donald Rumsfeld

WEEKLY PLANNER

MON

TUE

WED

THU

FRI

SAT

SUN

WEEK OF

TOP TASKS

NOTES

"Think ahead. Don't let day-to-day operations drive out planning."
- Donald Rumsfeld

WEEKLY PLANNER

MON

TUE

WED

THU

FRI

SAT

SUN

WEEK OF

TOP TASKS

NOTES

"Think ahead. Don't let day-to-day operations drive out planning."
- Donald Rumsfeld

WEEKLY PLANNER

MON

TUE

WED

THU

FRI

SAT

SUN

WEEK OF

TOP TASKS

NOTES

"Think ahead. Don't let day-to-day operations drive out planning."
- *Donald Rumsfeld*

WEEKLY PLANNER

MON

TUE

WED

THU

FRI

SAT

SUN

WEEK OF

TOP TASKS

NOTES

"Think ahead. Don't let day-to-day operations drive out planning."
- *Donald Rumsfeld*

WEEKLY PLANNER

MON

TUE

WED

THU

FRI

SAT

SUN

TOP TASKS

NOTES

"Think ahead. Don't let day-to-day operations drive out planning."
- Donald Rumsfeld

WEEKLY PLANNER

MON

TUE

WED

THU

FRI

SAT

SUN

WEEK OF

TOP TASKS

NOTES

"Think ahead. Don't let day-to-day operations drive out planning."
- Donald Rumsfeld

WEEKLY PLANNER

MON

TUE

WED

THU

FRI

SAT

SUN

WEEK OF

TOP TASKS

NOTES

"Think ahead. Don't let day-to-day operations drive out planning."
- *Donald Rumsfeld*

WEEKLY PLANNER

MON

TUE

WED

THU

FRI

SAT

SUN

WEEK OF

_____

TOP TASKS

_____

_____

_____

_____

NOTES

_____

_____

_____

_____

_____

_____

_____

"Think ahead. Don't let day-to-day operations drive out planning."
- Donald Rumsfeld

WEEKLY PLANNER

MON

TUE

WED

THU

FRI

SAT

SUN

WEEK OF

TOP TASKS

NOTES

"Think ahead. Don't let day-to-day operations drive out planning."
- *Donald Rumsfeld*

WEEKLY PLANNER

MON

TUE

WED

THU

FRI

SAT

SUN

TOP TASKS

NOTES

"Think ahead. Don't let day-to-day operations drive out planning."
- Donald Rumsfeld

WEEKLY PLANNER

MON

TUE

WED

THU

FRI

SAT

SUN

WEEK OF

TOP TASKS

NOTES

"Think ahead. Don't let day-to-day operations drive out planning."
- Donald Rumsfeld

WEEKLY PLANNER

MON

TUE

WED

THU

FRI

SAT

SUN

WEEK OF

TOP TASKS

NOTES

"Think ahead. Don't let day-to-day operations drive out planning."
- *Donald Rumsfeld*

WEEKLY PLANNER

MON

TUE

WED

THU

FRI

SAT

SUN

WEEK OF

TOP TASKS

NOTES

"Think ahead. Don't let day-to-day operations drive out planning."
- Donald Rumsfeld

WEEKLY PLANNER

MON

TUE

WED

THU

FRI

SAT

SUN

WEEK OF

TOP TASKS

NOTES

"Think ahead. Don't let day-to-day operations drive out planning."
- *Donald Rumsfeld*

WEEKLY PLANNER

MON

TUE

WED

THU

FRI

SAT

SUN

TOP TASKS

NOTES

"Think ahead. Don't let day-to-day operations drive out planning."
- Donald Rumsfeld

WEEKLY PLANNER

MON

TUE

WED

THU

FRI

SAT

SUN

WEEK OF

TOP TASKS

NOTES

"Think ahead. Don't let day-to-day operations drive out planning."
- Donald Rumsfeld

WEEKLY PLANNER

MON	
TUE	
WED	
THU	
FRI	
SAT	
SUN	

WEEK OF

TOP TASKS

NOTES

"Think ahead. Don't let day-to-day operations drive out planning."
- Donald Rumsfeld

WEEKLY PLANNER

MON

TUE

WED

THU

FRI

SAT

SUN

WEEK OF

TOP TASKS

NOTES

"Think ahead. Don't let day-to-day operations drive out planning."
- Donald Rumsfeld

WEEKLY PLANNER

MON

TUE

WED

THU

FRI

SAT

SUN

WEEK OF

TOP TASKS

NOTES

"Think ahead. Don't let day-to-day operations drive out planning."
- Donald Rumsfeld

WEEKLY PLANNER

MON

TUE

WED

THU

FRI

SAT

SUN

TOP TASKS

NOTES

"Think ahead. Don't let day-to-day operations drive out planning."
- Donald Rumsfeld